Yoruba Folktales

by
Amos Tutuola

Illustrated by Kola Adesokan

Ibadan University Press

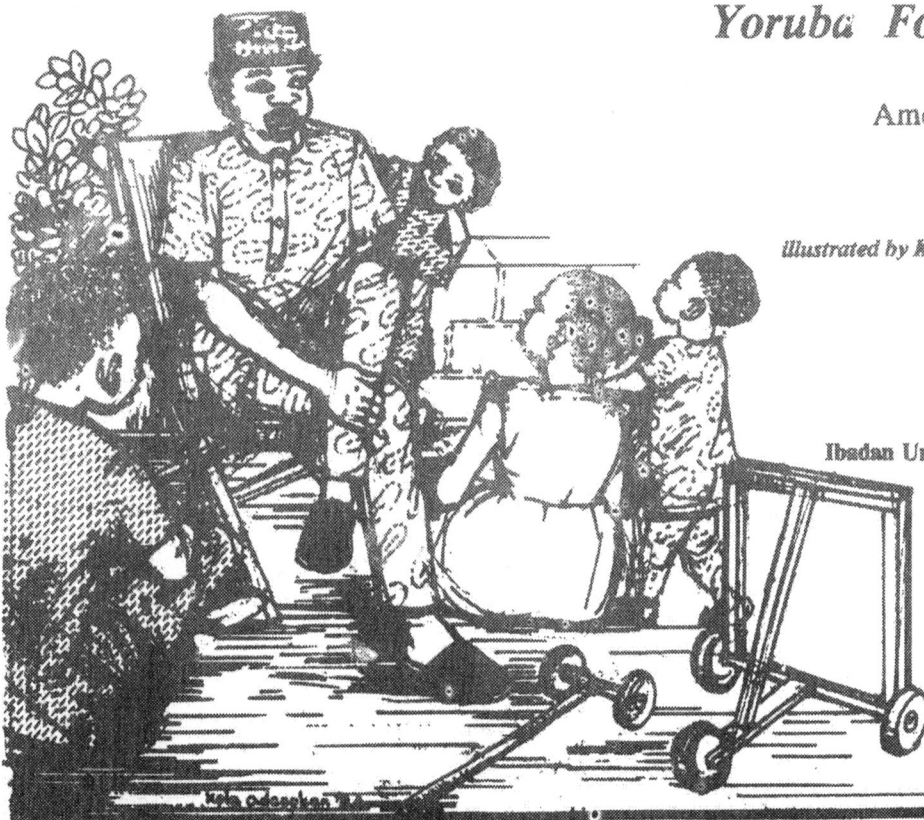

Ibadan University Press
Publishing House
University of Ibadan
Ibadan, Nigeria.

ISBN 978 121 186 5
Cover illustration by 'Bayo Ogundele of Ile-Ife, Nigeria.
Artwork and Layout: Kolawole Tony Adesokan.

CONTENTS

ACKNOWLEDGEMENT

Ibadan University Press wishes to express its gratitude to the Ford Foundation for subsidizing the publication of this special book.

We also wish to thank Professor Robert Wrenn for putting us in contact with Amos Tutuola, and for some editorial work he did on the manuscript.

AJANTALA, THE NOXIOUS GUEST, IS BORN

A long time ago, there lived in a town a woman trader. She was a trader of petty articles. She used to go from one forest to another when going to the markets. Her town was also in the heart of the forest. Her going from one market to the other every day did not prevent her from becoming pregnant. But to the surprise of the people of the town, she was unable to deliver her pregnancy for twenty-six years. This was not only a burden for her but also a great grief to her.

One morning, as she was on her way to the market, something knocked in her womb heavily several times. She was shocked in fear and then she slowed down her movement. She heard a strange voice coming out from her womb: "My mother! My mother! My mother!" Her pregnancy shouted from her womb. "I am not an ordinary child at all!" The pregnancy cried to the woman, Adedoja, with a sharp voice.

"What kind of a child are you then?" Adedoja asked with fright.

"I am a noxious* guest who is not going to stay with you, and my real name is AJANTALA!"

"Ajantala, the Noxious Guest?" Adedoja screamed in fear as she repeated the name.

"Yes, you are right. You shall call me Ajantala as soon as you have born me!"

Adedoja begged earnestly with fear. "Oh, let the time come quickly because you have kept yourself too long in my womb and that has been a terrible burden."

"I have been too long in your womb? How many years now have I been staying in your womb? Tell me now!" the pregnancy asked, shouting horribly from Adedoja's womb.

* Noxious = harmful, poisonous

1

"You have spent twenty-six years in my womb already, and the people of the town mock me and never sympathise with me!" Adedoja explained painfully to her talking pregnancy.

"And what kind of burden have I been to you?" wondered the pregnancy.

"It is too great and strange for me to express!"

"You are a fool to tell me that I have been a terrible burden! You have not even experienced what are called burdens. Just wait and see how troublesome a child I am when you have borne me!"

At this time, Adedoja did not know that an old woman was following her and that the old woman had heard the exchange of hot words between Adedoja and her pregnancy. This old woman asked with great surprise: "But with whom are you talking hotly like that?" Adedoja squirmed with fear when she looked behind her and saw the old woman.

"You — you — you see, my pregnancy is talking to me from my womb and I am really confused about the kind of preg —!"

The pregnancy hastily stopped Adedoja and warned her, "Shut up your mouth there and don't tell my secret to anyone! This old woman is a treacherous person. A villain she

2

is. Don't tell her the truth!''

Adedoja declined to tell the truth to the old woman. "Oh, thank you, my mother. But I am talking to myself!'' She feared her pregnancy's warning.

"What are you telling me? Are you in your dotage?* I have heard clearly that you were talking with somebody!'' the old woman said in anger.

"Hmm. Well, I am talking to . . . !'' Adedoja stammered.

Adedoja's pregnancy cautioned her once more, "Beware of yourself. Otherwise I shall show you the kind of a noxious child that I am. I have been lenient with you!''

Having heard the voice of this talking pregnancy again, the old woman was so afraid that she stopped immediately asking questions of Adedoja.

Adedoja and the old woman went on to the market. As soon as Adedoja had sold her wares and bought new ones, she returned to the town.

Adedoja had hardly walked heavily to the door-way of her house when her talking pregnancy shouted to the people of the house: "Eh, you people of the house, come and help my mother put her wares down!''

The people ran to Adedoja. They looked here and there with surprise and fear, but they did not see the person who had shouted to them. However, they helped Adedoja put her wares down.

"The voice that we heard was that of a man and not of a woman!'' the people remarked with surprise as they craned their necks and fastened their eyes on Adedoja in confusion.

"Can a pregnancy talk?'' one of the people asked.

I have not yet heard in my life that a pregnancy talks like a person,'' another one of the people said, hoping to clarify the confusion. But it did not help because Ajantala, the Noxious Guest, continued to threaten Adedoja every day.

One morning, at the very moment that Adedoja's pregnancy was exactly twenty-six years old in her womb, she was delivered of a strange male child before the people of the house.

"Ah, what a strange child is this? He has teeth in his mouth, bushy hair on his chin, and his moustache is full of bushy long hair. His eyes are as sharp and big as those of an old man, his head is full of plenty and strong hair and his chest is hairy!'' The people of the

*Dotage — weakness of mind and body due to old age

3

house clapped with panic and shouted.

The people were still looking at him confusedly when he stood and shouted suddenly: "Eh, my mother, tell the people that my name is Ajantala and that my nick-name is *Noxious Guest*". Willing or not, Adedoja announced his name and nick-name to the people.

"Ah, Ajantala, the Noxious Guest, welcome to the world!". However, the people showed that they despised his strange name by repeating it in derision.

Then in the presence of the people, Ajantala stood up again by himself and shouted: "Eh, my mother, give me the sponge. I am going to wash my body. It is too dirty!" Then after washing he asked for clothes and Adedoja, who was supposed to be his mother, hastily gave him the clothes. And he wore all as the people folded their arms and looked at him in fear and confusion.

Then, he went to the sitting room. He sat on a chair and then he shouted: "Eh, give me food and cold water. I am hungry badly!" After he had swallowed the food and drunk the water, he shouted, "Show me the way out!" The people hastily parted to the left and right and he passed between them to the door-way. But as he peeped outside, he shouted: "Ha — ah! Look. the dung of the domestic animals is everywhere on the ground. Of course, I am not

4

going to stay even a night in this dirty town! No! Not I!" As Ajantala was still shouting, hundreds of people heard his fearful voice and they ran to him. They stood in front of him and fastened their eyes on him. Everyone began to shout: "Ah, no doubt, this is not a human being. He must be an evil spirit!"

These people were right; Ajantala was one of the evil spirits. He lived inside the Iroko tree which was at the roadside on which Adedoja used to travel to the market. Unfortunately, one morning, as Adedoja was going to the market, she trekked by the Iroko tree, Ajantala, the Noxious Guest, came out from the tree and entered her womb. He lurked there just to rest for twenty-six minutes.

In fact, Ajantala spent twenty-six years in Adedoja's womb. But twenty-six years for the human beings were twenty-six minutes for the evil spirits.

Ajantala had hardly walked to the front of the house when he saw a group of red people who were playing 'ayo'.* He ran to them and he took the 'ayo' board suddenly and flung it far away. Then be abused them: "You hopeless old people, sitting down and playing 'ayo' in this dirty ground".

The old people stood up at once and shouted angrily:

"You are a stupid fool! You, an ugly small boy like you, are insulting us like that!" Ajantala without hesitation, slapped one of the old people on the face. Having seen him do so, the other people who surrounded the players of 'ayo' and were looking at them, started at once to beat him and he started to beat them in return.

But it was not easy at all to defeat Ajantala for he was as strong as iron. And within a few minutes, news had spread to every part of the town that a small strange man was beating a group of people. And thousands of people ran to the scene of the fight. They joined the other people and all were beating him. Yet, they could not overpower him.

When Ajantala had beaten more than one hundred people to death, all of the "Babalawo"* of the town came with their different kinds of magic spells to the scene of the tussle. With great anger, they drove Ajantala away from the town by means of their magic spells which were mainly prepared for driving away the evil spirits like Ajantala.

*Ayo = a traditional Yoruba game using seeds and a game board.

*Babalawo = a priest of Ifa; Ifa is a god of divination

5

AJANTALA AND THE THREE BROTHERS

Now, Ajantala, the Noxious Guest, started to roam about from one forest to another, looking for those he could live with as his fresh prey. One day, he saw a rough hut in a distance. When he got to it, he met in it three fellows who were the occupants of it. He entered and greeted them:

"Good afternoon to you all here!"

"Hello, good afternoon, old chap!" the lion, the tiger and the he-goat, who were the occupants, replied.

"Please, I shall be grateful if you will allow me to live with you as your guest. I promise, if you kindly allow me to be your guest, I shall teach you many things within a few days!" Ajantala, the Noxious Guest, thus begged and tricked the lion, tiger and he-goat, who were in those days human beings and were born of the same father and mother.

"With pleasure, we agree for you to be our guest", the lion replied.

"I thank you all very much. Ah, I am grateful!" Ajantala said with smiles, and then he sat down.

"But you must be a good guest to us!" the tiger warned.

"Oh, don't worry about that. You will soon know that I am indeed a wonderful guest!"

"But what is your name, my friend? You look hostile and cunning." The he-goat suspected Ajantala and he was right.

"My name is Ajantala. But the sons of men like you belittle me by calling me 'The Noxious Guest'. But I am not noxious in any way." Ajantala replied, pretending to be a nice and shy fellow.

"But will you be our servant?" asked the tiger. "Do you agree to that?"

"Ah, why, with pleasure. I agree to be your servant!" Ajantala promised as he was pulling the long hair of his chin.

"But Ajantala, if I am not mistaken, you

7

look older than your size or stature? Why?''
He-goat fastened his eyes on him, for he was
confused.

''You know, I have not had anything to eat
since a few days ago and that is why I have
shrunk to the small size you see now!''. As he
replied, he was scratching his head in a way
that showed he was telling a lie.

The lion, the tiger and the he-goat were
happy to have Ajantala as their guest and
servant. So the tiger stood up, and he brought
food and water to Ajantala. He ate the food
and drank the water to his satisfaction.

The following morning, it was the tiger's
turn to go and fetch their food from the bush.
He gave one big basket to Ajantala: ''Ajantala, take this basket and let us go and fetch
our food''. Without argument, Ajantala took
the basket and followed the tiger to the bush.
When the tiger had filled up the basket with
yams, he told Ajantala to carry it. This time,
Ajantala showed the tiger that he was noxious.
He slapped at tiger's eyes suddenly. The tiger
fell down helplessly at once. Before he was
again conscious, his eyes and face had swollen
up so much that he could hardly see.

''Why did you slap at my eyes and face? I
shall show you that I am a tiger'', the tiger
shouted angrily.

''What are you going to do to me? You,

8

hopeless man who has turned into a beast, as you are!'' Ajantala stood ready to fight and shouted terribly. Without hesitation, the tiger gave him a number of heavy knocks on the forehead with his fist. This did nothing to Ajantala. Instead, he became more noxious. He raised the whole of the tiger up and he threw him into a nearby rough ditch. The tiger was so wounded that he was unable to come out from the ditch. Ajantala went into it and dragged him out.

"Bend down! Bend down! And let me put the basket of yams on your head! You hopeless thing!'' Ajantala forced the tiger to carry the basket of yams. "Now, tiger, I warn you. You must not tell the lion and the he-goat that I threw you into the ditch, but tell them that you fell into it by mistake! Do you hear?''

"I hear,'' the tiger replied with a weak voice.

But when the tiger had carried the basket nearly to the hut, Ajantala took it from his head and put it on his own head. Then he carried it to the hut as if he had carried it right from the bush.

"Ah! Ah! But tiger, why are your eyes and face swollen up like this, and why is blood dripping from every part of your body?'' the lion and the he-goat shouted, astonished.

"Hmm. I fell into the ditch by mistake,'' the

tiger replied sluggishly. Ajantala had fastened his sulky eyes on him lest the tiger should tell them that he had slapped and thrown him into the ditch.

Ajantala treated the lion and the he-goat badly in the same way when he followed them to the bush on different occasions. Now, the tiger did not know that it was Ajantala who had wounded the lion and the lion did not know that it was Ajantala who had wounded the tiger and so too the he-goat. Thus Ajantala, with his cunning, wounded the three fellows.

At last, however, the three fellows knew that it was Ajantala who had hurt each of them. And they also knew that Ajantala was the most clever noxious guest that they had ever received into their hut.

By this time, Ajantala was the great fear of fears for the tiger, the lion and the he-goat. One night, when they thought that Ajantala was fast asleep, they sat down and began to plan how they would escape to save their lives.

"Ajantala is a cruel person," the tiger whispered painfully to the lion and he-goat.

The lion supported the tiger, "he is exactly like that. But we must try one way or the other to escape to somewhere now."

"But how can we escape from him without his seeing us?" the he-goat asked confusedly.

"If he sees us when we are escaping, he will follow us and then he will hurt us even to the point of death," the tiger said, for he was afraid.

"I suggest that as he is already fast asleep, it will be safe to pack all our food into the big basket and cover it with the rest of our belongings," the he-goat said. "And then we can escape with it to somewhere in the faraway forest." He glanced at Ajantala just to be sure that he was still asleep.

"Your suggestion is good," the lion and the tiger whispered.

"Let us pack our food and our other belongings at once," the tiger whispered.

"And when we have got everything ready, we shall have a short sleep before we start our journey," the lion whispered fearfully.

They stood up, they packed all their food which they had wrapped with leaves inside the basket and they put also all of their clothes on top of the food. After, they lay near the basket and they were fast asleep at once.

Unfortunately, Ajantala who they thought was asleep, was not asleep at all. But he heard all that they had planned to do. Ajantala was very cunning as well as noxious. As he was as small as a baby one year old, it was quite easy for him to enter the basket and hide himself at the bottom of it. Then he expected them to

carry the basket together with him to their proposed hiding place.

It was hardly after mid-night, when the tiger, the lion and the he-goat woke up and were so impatient that they did not bother to see whether Ajantala was still sleeping or not. And Ajantala was speechless and motionless inside the basket when the tiger and the lion hastily put the heavy basket on the he-goat's head. Thus, the three of them started their journey without knowing that Ajantala was inside the basket.

"Yes, we are quite safe now from cruel Ajantala!" shouted the tiger happily, as soon as they had travelled a bit far from their hut.

"Ajantala is so noxious!" the lion added with a smile.

"Perhaps Ajantala is not a human being as we were before!" the he-goat said with suspicion.

The lion said, "I am afraid, Ajantala must be a noxious immortal being. His strange bushy bead and long bushy moustache and his small size prove him to be so!" The lion spoke loudly and he was fairly correct.

"But I am sure he is one of the evil spirits who live inside the trees!" said the he-goat quite loudly. He had reconsidered Ajantala's appearance, and he was very correct.

Now, the three of them were of one opinion

that there was no doubt, Ajantala was an evil spirit who lived inside the tree. But all of them were so afraid even at that moment that they looked behind with half an eye, just to see whether Ajantala was coming.

When they had travelled till twelve noon, the he-goat who carried the basket of food, stopped suddenly and said:

"Now, my comrades, I must stop here to relieve myself. You go along and I shall catch up with you soon!" He-goat put the basket of food down. He stole from the food and ate it to his satisfaction. After, he put the basket back on his head and then he walked faster and caught up with them.

"Ah, woe unto Ajantala, the Noxious Guest and the son of the evil spirit!" The he-goat cursed Ajantala with a relieved voice when he remembered how the spirit had hurt him badly. But Ajantala heard him as he hid inside the basket on the he-goat's head.

"If Ajantala is a mortal being, he will not die better!" the lion shouted painfully as he examined the spots where Ajantala had hurt him badly. He did not know that Ajantala heard him.

"Now, comrades, it is sure now that we have escaped successfully from Ajantala, the Noxious Guest. But as that is sure, let us stop under this tree and eat from our food!" the tiger said cheerfully.

"Yes, you are right, tiger. I am badly hungry and tired!" the lion agreed.

They stopped under one big tree. They put the basket of food down and all sat round it. They did not know that Ajantala, the Noxious Guest, was hiding inside the basket and that he had heard them as they cursed and abused him along the way.

The tiger fastened his sulky eyes on the he-goat and shouted angrily, "What? Somebody has eaten from this food!".

"He-goat must be the one who has eaten from it when he stopped to relieve himself some minutes ago!" the lion shouted with anger as he too fastened his eyes on the he-goat.

But as the lion and tiger were sulky and stared at the he-goat, he denied the charge loudly: "No! I have not stolen from the food at all. If I did, then let something bring Ajantala to us now and judge the case for us!"

The he-goat had hardly mentioned Ajantala, when Ajantala jumped from the bottom of the basket into their circle, and all of a sudden, the tiger, the lion and the he-goat were so afraid that they scattered to different places.

The lion fled to a far country and there he has lived ever since. The tiger fled to a faraway

13

forest and there he has lived ever since. The he-goat fled to the town and thus he has been one of the domestic animals since that day.

That was how Ajantala, the Noxious Guest, separated the lion, the tiger and the he-goat from one another, although the three of them were once, in the days gone by, born of the same father and mother.

As soon as Ajantala had eaten the whole food, he started to roam about in the jungles and forests, looking for another living creature or human being whom he would punish to his satisfaction and then return to the Iroko tree inside of which was his place of abode.

ANTERE, THE CHILD OF
THE GODDESS OF THE RIVER

A long time ago, a man and his wife lived for several years of marriage without any child. They consulted several medical herbalists who prepared medicines for them which could make the wife, Olaoti, pregnant. All efforts were in vain. However, they were not fed up, and instead, they continued to go with sorrow from one medicine man to another till they were getting old.

Unfortunately, one day, they were told of one powerful medicine man who was also a good future-teller. This medicine man lived in a farway town. Nevertheless, they went to him, encountering several obstacles on the road before reaching the town. They met the powerful medicine man in his shrine and he told them to sit down.

"Yes, what is your problem?" the medicine man asked and then waited for a reply.

"Our problem is that, even though I married my wife many years ago, we have not even one child. So we have come to you for your help," the husband, Fijabi, explained sadly.

"Hmm. But the two of you were born barren," the medicine man, having cast his 'opele'* on the wooden bowl several times, explained to Fijabi and his wife, Olaoti.

"What? Born barren? Ah, please, medicine man, help us to get even one child!" the wife begged him impatiently and with tears.

"But my Ifa has disclosed that you and your husband were born barren!"

"But I want a child by all means. Even if it is born today and dies tomorrow, I don't mind!" the wife, Olaoti, insisted sadly.

The medicine man shook his head, astonished and he asked, "But what is the use then, when you get a child today and then it dies tomorrow?"

* *opele* is the chain used to tell the future.

15

"Please, just help me to get one by all means and I don't mind whatever happens to it!" Olaoti pleaded earnestly.

"Of course, I have the power to help you get a child. But that child will turn into sorrow in the end!" the medicine man warned the couple.

"Just help me get even one!" Olaoti, kneeling before the medicine man, begged.

"Now, I agree to help you. But I am going to kidnap for you the only remaining child of the goddess of the river. But the child will surely go back to her mother, the goddess of the river. At present, she has only one child with her. All the rest have gone to different barren women," the medicine man explained distinctly. "So, you must not allow the yet-to-come child," continued the medicine man, "to go and fetch water from the stream till when she has got married and has a child of her own."

After he had warned them about the yet-to-come child, he prepared a juju-soup for them. They took the juju-soup and returned to their town at once.

According to the medicine man's advice, Olaoti ate the whole soup the morning after they got back to their town. In fact, Olaoti got pregnant within a short period after she ate the

juju-soup. And after some months, she was delivered of a beautiful baby girl. With happiness, a strange name, ANTERE, was given to the baby when she was eight days old. The meaning of the strange name, ANTERE, was *the child which is kidnapped from the goddess of the river by means of juju'*.

Now, Antere continued to grow lovely, and the father and mother did not forget the warning of the medicine man who had told them that they must not allow her to go and fetch water from the stream until she was married and had got a child.

But unfortunately, when only five days remained before Antere was to go to her husband's house, and after everything for the marriage ceremony was ready, including the drummers, singers, flatterers and such for the ceremony, and as Antere's father and mother, friends and neighbours were in full merriment and all the other people of the town were waiting impatiently for the day to come, Antere, that morning, said to her father and mother, "My father and mother, I am going to the stream to wash my kitchen clothes." They did not object to her request for they thought she was at this time old enough and that she was free to go to the stream or anywhere else.

Then Antere collected all her kitchen-clothes together. She took one wooden bowl, she carried all to the stream to wash them. But as she knelt down and started to wash the clothes in the bowl, the goddess of the river appeared on top of the flowing water. Then the strong tides pushed her to Antere who was already paralysed with fear. As soon as the goddess touched Antere with her hand, she and Antere were drowned. Thus, she took Antere to her dwelling place which was under that river.

Antere's father and mother waited and waited for their only daughter to return but she did not. They went with tears to the stream but Antere was not seen there. They made every possible effort to know where she was but failed. In accord with the tradition of the town, they went to the king. When they informed him of their missing daughter with tears, without hesitation, the king sent some of his messengers to the stream. Yet Antere was not found at the stream.

But the following morning, when a woman went to the stream, she saw Antere's bowl floating on the surface of water. As soon as the woman told the king of this, the king again hastily sent one of his messengers to the stream to see whether it was true that Antere's wooden bowl was on the water.

Indeed, the messenger saw the wooden bowl floating on the surface of the water but he did not see Antere herself. He called loudly:

"Antere! Antere! Antere! Where are you! Come out now!" Alas! Instead of Antere, it was only Antere's enchanting voice that the messenger heard with a strange music. The music and Antere's voice were so enchanting that the messenger could not stand still but he began to dance from the stream to the palace of the king like a mad man.

As soon as he was forced by the people to stop dancing, he told the king: "In truth, I saw Antere's wooden bowl floating about on the water. But the worse of it was that the music and Antere's voice which came out from the bottom of the stream were extremely enchanting."

The king was so astonished that he invited all of his counsellors and the multitude of people of the town into his palace at once. He and his counsellors wanted to ride their horses to the stream, but the messenger warned: "Please, I pray, don't attempt to ride horses to the stream!"

"But why should we not ride our horses to the stream?" the king shouted horribly.

"Because the horses, as animals, will not be able to control themselves once they hear the enchanting music and Antere's enchanting voice!" the messenger explained.

"No! We shall ride the horses to the stream!" the king insisted, disregarding his

18

messenger's warning.

He and his counsellors mounted their horses stubbornly at once and all were riding the horses towards the stream while a multitude of people, including Antere's father and mother, followed them.

The troop got to the stream, and as soon as one of the messengers of the king shouted loudly: "Antere! Antere! Antere!" Antere answered loudly from the bottom of the stream with her usual enchanting voice. At the same time, the enchanting music started. The king, his counsellors, Antere's father and mother, and the multitude of people of the town began to dance to the enchanting music as if they were lunatics.

They continued to dance here and there at the bank of the stream. The king and his counsellors crushed several children to death with their horses. Seeing this, the parents of the children became so angry that they started to beat the king and his counsellors with sticks. Within a few minutes, several counsellors were beaten to death in this sudden and terrible fight.

When the king, his remaining counsellors and the people became conscious, the enchanting music stopped suddenly. They all returned to the town with grief for missing Antere.

Thus the Goddess of the River took Antere,

her child, back. But of course, the medicine man who was also a good future-teller, had forewarned, the barren wife, Olaoti and her husband, Fijabi, that it was 'the sorrow' which would be their only gain at the end, for they had neither a child in heaven nor on earth.

As he was carrying Olubi, the boy woke from sleep and he started to shout the name of the gate-keeper loudly: "Osoluga deliver me from this evil spirit! He is carrying me away! My father, mother, slaves and all of the domestic animals who were guarding me did not make any noise! Please Osoluga, the gate-keeper, save me!" That was the way that Olubi, the indulged son, lamented continuously while the evil spirit carried him to the gate.

"Eh, open the gate for me to pass, you, the gate-keeper!" The evil spirit shouted horribly with a strange huge voice.

Now, Osoluga, the brave gate-keeper, who had heard Olubi's lamentation, stood up and asked the evil spirit fearlessly: "Eh, stop there! Where are you carrying the boy to?"

"I am carrying him to the place of my abode in the forest. But just open the gate for me to pass!" the evil spirit shouted angrily.

Osoluga was so annoyed that he snatched Olubi suddenly from the spirit and he threw the boy into a huge bag which he hung on the left shoulder. Then he started to fight the evil spirit.

As the gate-keeper was strong, he was a match for the evil spirit. The fight was so fierce that they had smashed everything on the ground into pieces within a few minutes. Each

25

of them was entirely drenched with perspiration. Yet they could not defeat each other.

After a while, Osoluga, the gate-keeper threw one of his eight gourds of spells onto the ground. It changed the mid-night into the day at once. The evil spirits do not like the day time. This evil spirit hastily threw one of his seven gourds of spells onto the ground and then the day was changed back into night immediately.

Then they continued their fierce fight. The evil spirit was fighting the gate-keeper very gallantly in order to take Olubi back from him. But the gate-keeper did not allow him to do so.

Again, the gate-keeper threw one of his gourds of spells onto the ground and it changed the mid-night into the day. Without hesitation, the evil spirit, too, threw one of his gourds of spells onto the ground and it changed the day into the mid-night at once. So the fierce fight continued.

Each of them threw his gourds of spells onto the ground until all of the seven gourds of spells which the evil spirit had were finished. But the gate-keeper still had one. His own gourds of spell were eight in all, which is an even number, which is favourable for human beings.

Then he threw it onto the ground, and as soon as the mid-night had changed into the day, the evil spirit who had used all of his seven gourds of spell disappeared into the forest at once.

That is how the gate-keeper defeated the evil spirit, because he had had seven gourds, the odd number being favourable to the spirits.

Then the gate-keeper, Osoluga, took Olubi to his father and mother. They were so happy that they nearly gave all of their wealth to the gate-keeper, Osoluga.

Olubi had nearly died of wounds inflicted all over his body by the evil spirit. Nevertheless, his father and mother wisely stopped indulging him from that day.

THE ELEPHANT WOMAN AND THE HUNTER

There lived in a village a hunter named Oguntolu. Oguntolu the hunter, had two wives and many children. He was the best hunter of every kind of beast ever produced in his village.

As he was doing every morning, Oguntolu hung his hunting bag and matchet and gun on his left shoulder. Then he went direct to the jungle. When he got to the jungle, he saw a tree. The tree had plenty of branches on top and plenty of broad leaves. The hunter climbed the tree to the top and hid in ambush under the leaves. Then he watched for animals.

A few hours later, he saw an elephant coming towards a mighty mahogany tree. The tree had many big buttresses which were just like rooms. As Oguntolu, the hunter, was just getting ready to shoot at the elephant, he saw that it stopped in front of the mahogany tree. All of a sudden, the elephant took its skin away from its body. Hardly had it done so when it changed into the most beautiful woman that he had ever seen in his life. At this time, he was about to shoot at the woman, but he was prevented from doing so by the beauty of the woman.

Without wasting time, this beautiful elephant woman hid her skin inside one of the buttresses of the mahogany tree. Then she brought out from the same buttress a bundle containing a very beautiful dress. Having dressed up neatly, she took a beautiful covered calabash out from the buttress. She removed the cover of the calabash and the hunter saw inside it camwood-ointment, face powder, wrist-bracelets, beautiful neck-corals, earrings, antimony, and other fine things.

First, she rubbed the camwood-ointment all over her body, then she put the antimony on her eye-lashes very lightly. She rubbed the face powder all over her face and round her neck neatly. She put the beautiful coral beads on her neck and it reached to her breasts. After,

28

she put the bracelets on her wrists. Then she wound round her head a beautiful multi-coloured head-tie. Having done all that, she took out from the buttress a tin-covered calabash in which was very clear water. Having removed its cover, she looked at herself in the water. Having seen that she had dressed herself properly, she covered the tiny calabash in which there were camwood-ointment, antimony, wrist-bracelets and such in the same buttress. After that, she brought out from the same buttress a large wooden tray. Such provisions as roasted corn, roasted ground nuts, ripe bananas, ripe plantains and many confections were in that tray.

Having rearranged all of those provisions in the tray, she put it on her head and then she turned her back to the mahogany tree and started going to the market, which was on the outskirts of the hunter's village.

Now, this Elephant Woman became even more beautiful when she had dressed herself with all those things. And the hunter, as he still hid in ambush on top of the tree, was so attracted by the enchanted beauty of this woman that he wanted to shout:"Eh, beautiful woman, wait and follow me to my house!" But something hastily choked his throat at that moment.

Forcing himself to keep quiet, he followed

the Elephant Woman with his eyes until she had travelled in the jungle to such a distance that he could not see her any longer.

Soon after she had gone so far, the hunter came down from the top of the tree with his gun and matchet. With bravery, he went to the mahogany tree. He peeped into the buttress with fear. He took the skin of the Elephant Woman, he folded it, and then he went to his house with it. He climbed to the ceiling of his house and hung the skin there. As soon as he came down, he went to the market. He was surprised to see the Elephant Woman hawking her provisions about in the market and the people buying them from her.

After he had looked at her enchanted beauty for some minutes, he left the market and returned to the jungle. He climbed the tree and then he waited for the Elephant Woman to return.

As soon as the Elephant Woman had sold all of her provisions, she bought new ones. When the other people were returning to their respective villages and towns in the evening, she too left the market for the jungle.

When she got to the mahogany tree, she put her wooden tray loaded with the new provisions in the buttress carefully, but the hunter was looking at her from the top of the tree on which he hid himself. She peeped into the corner of the buttress hoping to bring out her elephant skin and wear it. To her dismay, she could not see it there. At first, she did not believe her eyes. The Elephant Woman raised her head up as if she were dreaming, wondering whether she had misplaced her skin. "But it is in this buttress I hid my skin," the Elephant Woman said, as if she was dreaming.

Again, she looked down, and with great confusion she searched every part of the buttress, yet she did not find it there. Now it was clear to this Elephant Woman that something strange had happened to her skin. Then she moved closely to the mahogany tree. She began to weep bitterly.

After a while and as tears were rolling down her cheeks, the hunter came down from the tree on which he had hidden. He went to her and asked her, as if he did not know anything about her skin, "Tell me, how did you manage to get into a dangerous jungle like this one, and what do you want in the buttress?"

"I come here to sell my provisions," the Elephant Woman murmured as she pointed her hand to her tray inside the buttress.

"To whom, in this jungle?" the hunter shouted, pretending to be amazed.

"To—to—to somebody," she stammered.

"Where is the someboldy? Show him or her to me now," the hunter insisted.

30

"Please, I beg you, give me back my skin, you who are a hunter," the Elephant Woman said. "I know you are the hunter who has taken it from the buttress. Do, as I beg you." The Elephant Woman knelt down before the hunter and begged earnestly with tears.

"You know, I have taken your skin and I shall not deceive you. But because I want you to be my wife, I shall not return it to you," the hunter said loudly with a smiling face.

"No! I cannot be your wife," the Elephant Woman shouted immediately, shaking her head.

"Why can't you be my wife?" the hunter asked softly.

"Because I belong to the animal-kingdom, and you belong to the human-kingdom."

"But that doesn't matter."

"Oh, that does matter a lot."

"All right, if you refuse to be my wife, you can stand there. I am going back to my village now. Goodbye!" the hunter pretended to go away.

"Ah, please don't go away and leave me here alone!" The Elephant Woman pulled the hunter back.

"Why?"

"Because I cannot return to my family in this form of a woman!" she explained with tears, still holding the hunter.

31

"If it is so, you must be my wife then. the hunter said simply.

"Have you wives at home?"

"Certainly, I have two!"

"Well it will be difficult for me to be your wife then!"

"In what way?"

"Because sooner or later, you will tell my secret to your wives."

"Not at all. I shall never tell your secret to anybody on earth!"

"You will," The Elephant Woman doubted his word.

"Believe me, I shall not. You know, it is strictly forbidden for hunters to tell secrets," the hunter promised as he was smiling and wiping tears away from the Elephant Woman's face.

"I see that your trap has caught me. Then let us go to your house."

From there, the Elephant Woman reluctantly followed the hunter to his house. And he showed her to his wives and told them also that she was his new wife.

"Oh, very nice. But where is her town or village?" his two wives asked suspiciously.

"Oh, her town is very far away. But don't bother to know her town anyway," the hunter replied simply.

For a few months, the two wives and the Elephant Woman lived comfortably. But after she gave birth to her first, second and third children, quarrels arose every day between the two wives and the Elephant Woman.

The two wives wanted to know from their husband, the hunter, by all means, the town or village from which he had brought the Elephant Woman. One day, as they knew that their husband was a drunkard, they bought many kegs of strong palm-wine for him. Soon he drank so much that he was unable to control himself.

Then when he fell down helplessly in his room, they went to him and asked: "By the way, from which town or village have you brought your new wife? Tell us now!"

"Oh, you mean that woman. She was an elephant and her skin is in the ceiling," the hunter said, telling the secret of the Elephant Woman to his other wives as a result of intoxication.

"Is that so?" The other wives wondered about what they had heard, and then they agreed to keep the secret in their minds as from that day.

"Oh, yes it is so," he confirmed as a result of intoxication. Then these two wives left the room.

After a few days, when the most senior wife and the Elephant Woman were quarelling, the

32

senior wife abused the Elephant Woman loudly: "Yes, be eating and drinking, your skin is hidden in the ceiling!"

When the Elephant Woman heard that her skin was hidden on the ceiling, she was confused. Perhaps their husband, the hunter, had told her secret to the other two wives. She became sluggish at once. But because she was an animal, she did not understand what was called "ceiling".

Thus the other two wives used to tell the Elephant Woman each time that they quarrelled, "Be eating and drinking, your skin is hidden in the ceiling."

One morning, soon after their husband had left for the farm, a serious quarrel arose between the same senior wife and the Elephant Woman again. As the senior wife usually abused the Elephant Woman, she again shouted terribly at her: "Be eating and drinking, your skin is in the ceiling!" But this morning, she pointed her hand to the ceiling of the house. And having seen where the hand pointed to, the Elephant Woman, understood this morning what was called "ceiling" and she saw where it was.

As soon as the Elephant Woman knew what was called ceiling and she saw where it was, she went high up and climbed into the ceiling at once. And, in fact, she saw her skin hanging

there. Without wasting a second, she wore her skin and she became an elephant immediately. Then she jumped onto the floor suddenly in the form of an elephant. As the two other wives screamed in fear, she tore them and their children into pieces. But she did not touch her own three children. Then she ran like a tiger to the hunter in the farm. She told him in the human voice:

"Well, you should take great care of my children! Goodbye!"

"Wait! Don't go away!" the hunter shouted.

"No! I cannot wait! You have told my secret to your two wives. Therefore, the elephant is going back to her elephant-kingdom. I am going home!" She was running towards the jungle. "And if it were not for my children, I would have torn you too into pieces!" Then she disappeared into the jungle at once.

"Please, forgive me!" the hunter begged, but he simply begged the jungle, for the animal had gone back to the animal-kingdom.

Now, the hunter knew that his wives had told the elephant where her skin was hidden. Then with anger he ran to the house but only burst into tears when he saw the dead bodies of his wives and their children on the floor.

"If I had known I would not have told the

secret of the Elephant Woman to my two
wives!'' Thus the hunter blamed himself at
last, but it was too late for him.

SEGI AND THE BOA-CONSTRICTOR

Long, long ago, there lived in a famous town a man named Olaogun and his wife, named Oyedara. They had only one daughter named Segi. They tried to have more children but they could not. They became old and weary.

In accord with the tradition of their land, Segi's father and mother went to the future-teller. They asked the wise man to help them find out from his Ifa, the god of divination, the future of their only daughter, Segi, all that which was required for her to do and not to do, and also what should be their behaviour towards her.

The wise man found out from his Ifa and then translated all that which his Ifa told him to Oyedara and Olaogun. He told them they must allow Segi to do all, whatever she wished to do.

Segi was so beautiful that her strange beauty attracted every young man who saw her at once. Everyone of them even prepared to marry her at once with whatever amount of money that might cost him. But alas! Segi would not agree to marry anyone of the young men. But then her father and mother noticed that Segi was getting near over-mature for marriage, all of her age group girls had got married long since.

They tried to force her to marry one man, although they knew that they had gone against her nature and the warning of the wise man (the future teller). Segi refused stubbornly to marry the man. At last, when they were fed up advising her to marry a man, they left her to herself.

There was an assembly field on the outskirts of this town, the circumference of which was more than three kilometres. The exhibitions of masquerades and plays such as wrestling, magic displays, and such things as were sports of the year, took place on this assembly field once a year. So innumerable people of this famous town and people from far distant towns, villages, and farms used to come to the field to witness the sports of the year. But as people were so numerous there was nobody who could identify which were the human beings and which were the immortal ghosts, evil spirits, beasts, and such who had turned into beautiful human beings when coming to witness these yearly sports.

Now, this day that the sports were taking place on the assembly field, Segi, her father and mother came as others did to witness these important yearly sports. But this day, Segi saw one man who was among the innumerable people.

"Ho, look at this beautiful man! I am going to meet him!" Segi pointed out the strange man to her father and mother and then she stood up. She began to push people left and right, and by doing so she was forcing her way to the man.

Segi's father and mother called her back, "Come, Segi, don't go to him!" But she did not listen to them. When she forced her way to the man, she held both his hands in a lovely way. She asked with a smiling face:

"I wish to be your wife now, gentleman!"

"Why do you wish to be my wife?" the strange beautiful man asked.

"Because of your strange beauty!" Segi twisted to him and she explained with smiles. "And I am ready to follow you to your town now!"

"But you cannot follow me to my town just today, the first day you see me. And it is forbidden in my town for a person to marry a lady the same day that he meets her," the strange man said. "And it is proper for you to acquaint me with your parents first before you can follow me to my town" he added softly.

"Never mind to see my parents for they never go against my wish!" Segi replied with a lovely voice as she fastened her eyes on the strange man.

"Please, don't try to follow me today," the strange man begged.

Segi answered impatiently, "But if your wish is to know my parents before you will allow me to follow you, my father and mother are on the assembly field, witnessing the sports as well!"

"I must know, what is your name?" the strange man asked.

"My name is Segi!"

"All right, take me to your father and mother." The strange man, having shrugged, followed Segi to her father and mother.

"Now, my father and mother, just for your information, this is my husband at last!" Segi showed the strange man to them. "And I am following him to his town now!"

Though Segi's father and mother were so extremely happy to see that their daughter agreed to marry a man at last, they were not happy that she would follow him the same day.

"Ah, we have not yet heard of a lady who had followed her intended husband to his house or town the same day that she met him. And Segi, you should wait for us to perform the necessary marriage ceremony for you", Segi's father and mother said.

"No! I cannot wait but I wish to follow him to his town now. Please I remind you of the warning of the wise man, that you must not go against my wish!" Segi shouted at her father and mother. Then she followed the strange man at once.

"It is true, Segi, you love me and you are following me now. Do you know the kind of a man that I am?" the strange man drawled his question.

"I am not bothered to know that, but I shall follow you to your town today," Segi insisted.

"But Segi, do you know where and how far my town is and what kind of parents I have?" The strange man tried to persuade Segi to change her mind.

"Wherever your town is, I shall follow you

there. And whatever your parents are, I shall live with them comfortably!'' Segi insisted, still following the strange man.

The beautiful strange man had tried his best to persuade Segi not to follow him but failed. So he allowed her to follow him. After Segi and the strange man had travelled far away from the assembly field, they came to a sea unexpectedly. Without hesitation, the beautiful strange man left Segi and ran into the sea. He had hardly dived when he changed into a very big boa-constrictor. Then the boa-constrictor glided onto one rock which was in the middle of the sea. And it raised its big head up and looked at Segi with its frightening eyes. Segi fastened her eyes on it, with great fear.

"What? That means the beautiful strange man is a boa-constrictor and not a human being as I have taken him to be! Ah, I am finished today! But who will save me now? And who will take me back to my father and mother? Ah, I am finished today!'' Segi began to blame herself and was lamenting loudly with tears as the boa looked at her, winking momentarily.

Soon, the fear of this boa forced Segi to start running away for her life. But the boa-constrictor jumped into the sea and it swam to her. Having coiled round her body, it swam back onto the rock. But Segi had fainted for fear before the boa glided onto the rock. And

38

it had hardly glided back onto the rock when it started to swallow Segi. But when it noticed that Segi made no motion or breath, it thought that she had died. Then it vomited her and glided away. Soon after, a strong breeze rushed onto Segi, she became conscious. Then she sat up on the rock. Having rested for a while, she propped her chin with her left hand. Then she started to lament until she fell asleep unnoticed. But hungr and the sounds of a herd of hippopotami, which were grazing about in the water, woke her in the midnight.

After a while the hippopotami grazed to the rock, though Segi feared them at first. But when she knew that she would simply die of hunger and cold if she kept herself any longer on the rock, she jumped fearlessly onto the back of one of the hippopotami. And as soon as the strong tides forced them to the sandy bank of the sea, she hastily jumped onto the bank. Then as it was already dawn at that time, she started to travel along on the sand. Fortunately, she did not travel far before she got to the bush which was on the outskirts of a small town. Within a few minutes she came to the town, although she had nearly collapsed from hunger before reaching there. Segi was so lucky that she saw a food-stall as soon as she begain to travel along in the town. She entered the food-stall at once and sat down wearily.

"Please, give me food and meat at once!"

39

Segi shouted to the food-seller without asking for the prices of the food and meat, though she had no money with her.

After Segi had eaten and drunk water to her satisfaction and rested for some minutes, she stood up. But when she moved to leave, the food-seller asked: "But you have not paid for the food and meat you have eaten. Please pay the money now!"

"Well, I beg you to forgive me, I have no money with me!"

"You have no what? After you have eaten my food and meat, you are just telling me that you have no money! You are just joking. You hopeless lady! Thief!" The food-seller frowned at her and held her firmly. Within a few minutes, many people ran to the stall. All began to beat Segi.

After a while the people shouted: "Let us take her to the king to give her severe punishment!" Then they dragged Segi to the king.

"But why did you not pay for the food and meat you have eaten, my dear lady?" the king boomed at Segi.

"Your worship. In fact I bought the food without having money in hand and I did so intentionally," Segi replied without shame.

"Why did you do so intentionally when you knew that the food and meat were not free sacrifices?" the king asked.

40

"It was the hunger which forced me to do so," Segi confessed.

"But tell me, from where did you come to this town?"

"Your majesty, the king, I shall tell my story now."

"All right, tell me your story now, my dear beautiful lady!"

"Well, in short, I saw one beautiful man on the assembly field of my town. I followed him, and as soon as I followed him to the sea, he turned into a big boa-constrictor. As I was running away for my life, it pursued me and caught me up in a moment. Then it took me to the rock which was in the middle of the sea. It had swallowed me up to a half, when it thought that I was dead and then it vomitted me and then left me on the rock and glided away.

As soon as I was conscious, I began to lament till when I fell asleep unnoticed. Hunger and cold woke me up. When a herd of hippopotami grazed near the rock I jumped onto the back of one of them and when the strong tides forced them near the bank of the sea, I jumped onto the sand and from there I started to find the way back to my town, but I came to this town instead.

"Because there was no money with me and I was nearly dead of hunger, I went to the food-stall and I bought the food and meat without paying for them." Segi thus explained her difficulties briefly to the king.

Now, the king and the crowd of people were sorry for Segi. The king did not punish her but he paid for the food and meat that she had eaten instead.

Segi's beauty had attracted the king as soon as he saw her, so he took her as his wife at once. Because Segi was born with a good manner and kind temper, the king loved her much more than any of his old wives.

Seeing this, all of the old wives began to treat Segi with ill-temper. They always made mockery of her that she was a foreigner who had no parents. Because of this, Segi was not happy for a single moment and she did not ever open her mouth and laugh.

As time went on, when those old wives noticed that Segi never opened her mouth and laughed, they believed that she had no teeth in her mouth and that was why she never laughed.

Now, it was a serious offence for any king who might reign in this town to marry a toothless lady. Knowing this and in order to get rid of Segi or to see that she was killed, those old wives of the king went to the counsellors secretly. They reported to them that their husband, the king, had married a toothless lady

Having heard this false report from them, the counsellors were greatly annoyed with the king. They knew the side effects that there would be in the town: epidemics of all kinds of diseases, sicknesses, and the people would have no peace of mind. Therefore the toothless wife must be killed.

The third day after those old wives had brought the false report to the counsellors, the counsellors went to the king. They told him angrily: "We, the counsellors of this town, order your majesty, the king, to gather your wives together at the palace in five days' time. When all of them are arranged in one row, then we shall call them one by one to sing and laugh to us and by doing so we shall discover one who is toothless among them and then we shall kill her at once, according to the law of our town". Then the counsellors went away angrily.

The king nearly ran mad immediately after the counsellors told him all that they were going to do for each of his wives in five days' time. For he was not sure whether or not one or more of his wives might be toothless. And those old wives who hated Segi were happy now when they had heard that the counsellors were going to give every one of them a test.

They started to tell one another with happiness that indeed Segi's death was imminent. But they had forgotten that the punishment of one who might tell a lie in their town was death.

When the day of the test was reached, all of the king's counsellors arrived at the palace in the morning. They ordered all of the king's wives to sit in one row. The most senior one was number one on the row while Segi sat on the extreme end. Thus all of them sat on the row according to their seniority. After that the king sat at the back of all looking worried.

Then the test started from the most senior wife who was number one on the row. The counsellors told her:

"Yes, you as the most senior wife of the king, sing and laugh now in the presence of us and the crowd of the people!" She sang and then she laughed and the whole assembly saw that she had teeth in her mouth. Then the counsellors ordered her to sit on a separate row. In the same way, the counsellors continued to examine all of the wives till it was Segi's turn. To the surprise of the other wives, when she sang and laughed loudly, the assembly saw teeth clearly in her mouth.

Having seen that Segi had teeth in her mouth, those old wives knew at once that they had put themselves in a serious trouble. Because of the death penalty, everyone of them wanted to save her life.

But that was impossible for they had told a lie against Segi. Ind d,eas there wase r al justice in this town, the counsellors, without respecting their king, sentenced all of those old wives to death at once. And then without hesitation, the king's executioners led them to the sacred-grave and then beheaded them in front of the god of iron for telling the lie.

After some weeks, the king, Segi and the counsellors went to Segi's father and mother in their famous town. The king paid Segi's dowry to her father and mother. They spent a few days with them. Then they returned with Segi to their town.

Some people were convinced someone was to be blamed for the punishments that Segi experienced. They questioned whether her father and mother had allowed her to do her wish. But many people also blamed her nature which had prevented her father and mother from rearing her in the right course.

THE SHELL-MAN AND THE
TERROR OF THE BUSH

Though the Shell-man, Tort, was really a handsome and promising young man, he was also cunning, the greatest deceiver, liar, talebearer, burglar and confusionist who ever lived in his land. And such things as pilfering and pick-pocketing were his leisure hours' sports.

Now, the Shell-man, Tort, worked for the god of the forest for the period of three years without any compensation, in respect of the offences which he committed.

Having served the three year servitude, he returned to his village and then he continued to live happily with his wife, Yanribo, the Beetle-woman and with their little child.

But one morning, the Shell-man, Tort, with his usual funny tricks told his wife: "Yes, Yanribo, I am going to pay a courtesy visit to your mother who is my mother-in-law, this morning."

"Oh, how happy I am," Yanribo, the Bettle-woman said cheerfully. "Please when you get there tell my mother to send some luxurious things to me. "

"All right, I leave now!" The Shell-man, Tort stood up and left the house for the village of his mother-in-law. Within a few hours, he trekked to the village.

Tort's mother-in-law received him with happiness: "Ah, I welcome you to my house, my son-in-law, the Shell-man and the man of all behaviours! Come and sit in the sitting room! How are your wife, the Bettle-woman, and your child? Hope all are well?" Shell-man was Tort's first name and Beetle-woman was Yarinbo's maiden name which Tort's mother-in-law had mentioned this morning. And the Shell-man, Tort, sat in the sitting room at once.

A few minutes later, delicious food was brought to the Shell-man. Tort, with his usual greed, ate the whole food without leaving even a bit of it for the children of the house to eat. And that was against the tradition of the people.

In the evening, when the Shell-man, Tort,

kola adesokan

was ready to return to his village, his mother-in-law gave him a large covered basin:

"Please, the Shell-man, give this porridge to your wife, the Bettle-woman!"

Tort, having thanked his mother-in-law, left the village. But he hardly trekked one kilometre, when he stopped at the roadside and shouted greedily to himself: "Ha! Not my wife alone will eat the whole of this very delicious porridge!" He removed the lid of the basin, looking at and sniffing the sweet smell of the porridge.

Then the Shell-man at once entered the bush. He sat under an Iroko tree. But the moment he began to eat from the porridge basin, he heard a horrible voice.

"Who is sitting there?" The voice came from the inside of the Iroko tree.

"I am," Tort replied with a faint voice.

"What do you want to do under me?"

"I want to eat from my wife's porridge".

"But that porridge belongs to your wife alone!" the voice reminded the Shell-man, Tort.

"Yes, of course, but I want to eat some of it and then I shall give the remainder to my wife".

"But why don't you go home with it and eat it along with your wife?" querried the voice.

"Well if I do so, I am afraid, perhaps my wife will not allow me to eat it with her," Tort replied.

"Of course, you are well known throughout the land by your behaviours. But will you allow my children to eat some of it with you?" the voice asked.

"How many are your children?" the Shell-man, Tort, asked as he raised his head up and was looking at the top of the Iroko tree sternly.

"My children are only four in all!"

"Ah, they are too many," the Shell-man distorted his face and exclaimed.

"All right, if you cannot allow my children to eat the porridge with you, leave where you sit now. And don't let me see you around here!" the voice shouted at Tort with annoyance.

Then the Shell-man, Tort, took the porridge and left there at once. Having travelled far from the Iroko tree, he saw a big rock. He stopped there and climbed up and he sat on it. But as he prepared to eat the porridge, he heard a horrible voice here again, which came out from the rock!

"Who sits on me there?"

"I am, the Shell-man, Tort", he replied and then hesitated.

"What do you want to do there?" the voice asked.

"I want to eat a bit from my wife's porridge".

"Will you give some of it to my children?" the voice asked.

"But how many are your children?" Tort asked with a greedy voice.

"They are not many. They are only up to forty in all!"

"Why! They are too many. I cannot give them from the porridge," the Shell-man shouted and without hesitating to hear more words from the rock, he started to eat the porridge with his usual greed.

"But for refusing to allow my children to eat from the porridge, let your groin cleave onto the rock!" the voice commanded aloud.

"That is your own problem and I am not concerned about that," the Shell-man said. Without paying heed to the voice's commands, he continued eating from the porridge.

After Tort had nearly eaten the whole porridge, he wanted to stand up and go away. But to his surprise and fear, he could not stand up because his groin adhered onto the rock.

He stood astride firmly and then he pulled. Now the Shell-man, Tort, was embarrassed and his groin began to pain him so much that he started to beg the rock to release him. At last when he realized that the rock did not listen to him, he began to shout for help Luckily, one giant-like ape who was passing through there at that time heard his shout Then he came there and climbed the rock at once.

"Ha! There your greediness has landed you," the ape said, first chuckling and making mockery of the Shell-man. "Okay, I shall help you," he said when he observed that Tort's groin had adhered onto the rock.

He stood astride firmly and then he pulled Tort with all his power. Unfortunately, the skin of Tort's groin tore on the rock. Then the rest of the groin began to pain him and he was unable to wait and thank the ape and he could not take the basin of the porridge along with him.

The Shell-man had hardly entered his house when he fell down and cried loudly for pain.

"But what has cut away your groin?" his wife, Yanribo, the Beetle-woman asked with fear.

Tort lied to his wife: "When I was returning to the house, I met the war of cutting groins on the road. But when I joined the war, the enemies cut some of my groin. Of course, I cut their own in return."

"But since when I was born, I have not heard of such a war called 'The war of cutting groins!' A war which is cutting only the groins

49

kola ladesokan

but not killing people," Tort's wife, the Beetle-woman remarked with wonder because she doubted Tort.

"Oh, there is the 'war of cutting groins'' but being a woman you cannot know or hear of it." The Shell-man, Tort, deliberately confused his wife.

Yanribo, the Bettle-woman, started to treat the sore of her husband's groin. And it was healed within a few days.

Now, the Shell-man, Tort, was well. But soon, he planned the way he could persuade his wife to give him the biggest of all her wethers* because she was rearing many animals.

"You see, Yanribo, my lovely Beetle-woman, the day before yesterday, when I went to the future-teller, he warned me that unless I sacrifice the biggest and fattest of your wethers to my head, I shall fall into the 'war of cutting heads' in the same way as I fell into the 'war of cutting groins' last time". The Shell-man, Tort, lied to his wife and then he hesitated to see her reaction.

Although Yanribo, the Bettle-woman, knew her husband, Tort, well, that he was greedy, treacherous, cunning, selfish, and all that, she agreed for him to sacrifice her wether to his head.

Then Tort stood up and caught the animal. He slaughtered it and his wife cooked all of it in a big pot at once.

"Yes, the animal is well cooked now. May I serve from it to our neighbours for they helped me cook the animal?" the Beetle-woman asked her husband.

Tort frowned at his wife, "No! No! Don't serve even a bit of it to anybody. The future-teller did not tell me to do so. But he told me to carry the whole of it to the grave of my father which is in the far bush!"

"Is that so? But that is not fair enough," Yanribo remarked with pain.

"Yes, it is so, But bend down and help me put the pot of the meat on my head. I am carrying it right now to the grave of my father in the bush!" The Shell-man, with his usual greediness, having hung his matchet on his shoulder, carried the pot of the meat into the bush. The Shell-man did all this so that he might eat all of the meat alone.

"Yes, this tree has plenty of shade, I will stop under it and eat my meat." Tort put the pot of meat down under the tree. But as he sat before the pot and was about to eat the meat, a small bush-rat went through there.

"Tort saw the small bush-rat and said, "Ah, this rat is another meat. I shall chase it and when I kill it, I shall eat it first and then my meat will follow!" He left his meat and started to chase a small rat along greedily.

As soon as the Shell-man had chased the rat

a short distance, it ran into a strange huge hole. The hole was so huge that a person could enter and walk easily into it. Tort ran into it, still chasing the rat along until he chased it to a fearful strange old woman. The rat ran to the old woman and it hastily climbed onto the old woman's lap. Then it stopped there and looked at the Shell-man with bad eyes.

This strange old woman sat on a mighty boa which coiled round like a hill. Tort screamed greatly immediately when he saw this strange woman and he began to shake with fear as he stood in front of her.

Though the old woman appeared to be an ordinarily woman, she was one of the cruel immortal creatures. She had very long whiskers but her head was bare. Her name was *Aworiwo,* the Terror of the Bush.

Aworiwo, the Terror of the Bush shouted angrily, "You the son of man! Are you so brave that you were chasing my bearer the bush-rat to kill it? This is an insult to me. But you will not go without a severe punishment!"

The Shell-man, Tort, answered with fear, "Please forgive me, I did not know that the rat is your bearer. I thought it is an ordinary rat like those which I had killed and eaten in the past. Please let me go back to the pot of my meat!"

"So you have killed and eaten a lot of my bearers! You are Tort the Shell-man, are you not?" Aworiwo, the Terror of the Bush had become angrier.

"Yes, of course, I did. But have pity because I did not know that all of the rats are your bearers. I beg, forgive me that!"

"But your offence is so serious that it deserves no forgiveness at all. But to punish you severely is the substitute you deserve, you hopeless greedy Shell-man!" Aworiwo, the Terror of the Bush would not pardon Tort, the Shell-man.

When Tort knew well that the Terror of the Bush refused to pardon him, with great fear, he turned his back to her and started to run to the outside of the huge hole.

"Let you, the Shell-man, Tort, be blind and your nostrils be locked forthwith!" the Terror of the Bush commanded with her magic voice. Tort immediately became blind and his nostrils were blocked. When he could not see and could not breathe in or out, he stopped. She commanded Tort to come near to her, and carry her on his head to the pot of his meat.

Willing or not, Tort obeyed and he staggered to her. As soon as he put her on his head, he regained his eyesight and breathed in and out as usual, so he could carry her to the pot of meat.

Then the Shell-man put Aworiwo down in front of the pot of his meat and she swallowed

kola adesokan

all at once without allowing greedy Tort to eat even a bit of it.

Having seen this, Tort wanted to return to his village with sorrow. "Tort, you have to carry me to your house!" Aworiwo said.

"No! I cannot carry a terrible immortal old woman like you to my village!" the Shell-man shouted angrily refusing to come back and carry her to his village.

"Is that so? All right, let your eyes be blind and your nostrils be blocked now!" The Terror of the Bush, Aworiwo, commanded.

When Tort could not see and could not breathe in or out, he staggered back to her. He put her on his head. And she had hardly touched his head when he regained his eyesight and could breathe in and out. Then he carried her to his village and he put her in one of his rooms. Thus the Shell-man, Tort, put trouble in his house as a result of his greediness.

Within a few hours, all the people of the village had heard that Tort had put the Terror of the Bush, the old woman with whiskers on both her cheeks, in his room. The people had been hearing of the strange old woman long ago and wanted to see what she looked like, so they ran to the Shell-man's house to see her.

As the crowd of people were looking at the strange and horrible appearance of Aworiwo, she shouted to the Shell-man: "Eh, Shell-man, Tort, tell the people to go and bring all their food for me!"

"You all the people! Aworiwo, the Terror of the Bush, said that you should go back to your houses and bring all your food for her!" the Shell-man told the people with fear. But all the people scattered as soon as Tort had delivered the message to them.

Nevertheless, Aworiwo ate all of the food that Tort and his wife, the Bettle-woman, had at home and she ate the whole food of the rest people of the village. Yet she continued asking them to bring more to her. Then the head of the village summoned an emergency meeting to decide how to destroy the Terror of the Bush.

"How can we free ourselves from Aworiwo, the Terror of the Bush?" the head of village asked.

"The best thing that we can do to save us is to desert the village!" one of the elders suggested.

"But Aworiwo will see us when we are leaving the village!" another one of the elders reminded the assembly.

"The best thing to do is to give plenty of the hot drink to the Terror of the Bush. But when she has drunk and she falls asleep, then we shall burn her together with the house!" the oldest man in the village suggested.

kola adesokan

"Yes, you are right." The other people agreed, "That is what we shall do!"

Without hesitation, they gave plenty of hot drink to Aworiwo and, as soon as she was fast asleep, Tort and his wife hastily removed all of their belongings to another house. The house was set on fire and Aworiwo was burnt to ashes. After the house had burnt to ashes along with Aworiwo, the Shell-man, Tort, suddenly remembered that he forgot to take all his money away along with other property.

Now, the people of the village were free from the Terror of the Bush, but the Shell-man, Tort, lost his house, his money and Aworiwo did not allow him to eat the wether which he took from his wife, Yanribo, the Beetle-woman, by his cunning. Thus, it has become a proverb since that day that "It is in the bush that the animal of the greedy person lives."